Almost

Heaven

Devotions For The
Journey Home

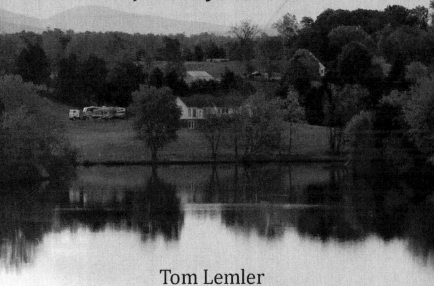

Tom Lemler

This book is
dedicated in memory of
my niece,
Breanna Sue Lemler.

Bre began her journey
on earth December 19, 1994
and arrived at her eternal
home on July 10, 2016.

Breanna's Song

By Tom Lemler

Sometimes the sorrow is hard to see past.
When the news hits you hard that today was her last.
The good parts of life are painful to see.
When all of a sudden they're just a memory.

But a life that's not lived is no life at all.
And she lived it full and always walked tall.
No words are enough, they surely will fail.
To erase all the sorrow of this chapter's tale.

She lived with such joy, she wanted it all.
Whether just living life or playing some ball.
Her faith was alive for all who would see.
She was loved by her friends and her whole family.

What would she say if she could still talk?
I think you can tell by the way she did walk.
Her life filled with joy was more than just fun.
She lived it daily, in step with God's Son.

And so in the sorrow of days yet ahead.
There's hope in the darkness of nights filled with dread.
The weeping and sorrow will last for a night.
But someday we'll gather in the heavenly light.

So what can we do as we mourn and grieve?
But to make sure we're ready for when it's our time to leave.
And when we all get there, I think we will see.
The beauty of heaven as we gather with Bre.

Almost Heaven:
Devotions For the Journey Home

Tom Lemler
Impact Prayer Ministry
2730 S Ironwood Dr
South Bend IN 46614
www.impactprayerministry.com
tlemler@gapministry.com

Each one of us is on a journey to our final, and eternal, destination. As Christians, we live with the confident assurance that our eternal home is with God. But, we're not home yet and there is a life to be lived as we journey toward heaven. It is my prayer that this devotional journal helps you discover not only a glimpse of heaven, but that it would prepare you to more fully live like you are home even as you continue the journey.

This book is dedicated in grateful acknowledgment to God who has called me to this journey toward my true home. I'm also thankful for the Association of College Ministries and their 2016 president, Danah Himes, for planting the seeds of this book in my mind with the theme of the 2016 National Student Conference, "Not Home Yet". I thank the Deer Run congregation and my family — each of them helps me in a great way to pursue the calling and gifting God has put in my life. To all of these, and to you my readers, thank you!

Table of Contents

Almost Heaven:

Introduction

Are we there yet? How much longer? While these questions are often attributed to young children, they are questions that are asked by children of all ages who are looking forward to a destination. As Christians, we long for our heavenly home but since we're not there yet, how can we make our current home more like the one we are headed toward? Through time in prayer, this devotional journal was written to help you understand, and live, some important traits of that future home while you journey toward it.

You may use this book as a thirty-one day devotional or go through it at whatever pace suits you. Take your time to let each statement about your home sink deeply into your being. The book is designed to be used as both a devotional and a journal as you discover what God says about you.

Each topic follows the same three-page format. The first page is simply a statement of that day's focus and a scripture reference to get you started in God's Word. Look up the scripture reference and meditate on God's Word about the home He is preparing.

The second page is some devotional writing that has come from my prayer time focused on that day's subject. It will include questions to help you think more clearly about preparing for a heavenly home. There will be direction and suggestions on how to focus your prayer time as you seek to grow in relationship with God. As you go through this page of each day's topic, spend time with God in prayer for yourself and for the people around you to have a greater grasp of living with an eternal perspective.

The third page is your turn to make this devotional even more personal! It contains a heading of the day's topic and then a blank lined page. This is for you to record your interaction with God each day. Jot down your thoughts, your prayers, other scriptures that God brings to mind during your time with Him, and/or changes in your attitude or actions that He reveals you need to make. Use this journal page to help you remember and to help you grow.

In prayer,
Tom Lemler
Impact Prayer Ministry

Day One

A Home

With Authority

(1 Peter 3:22)

A Home with Authority

When you think of authority, who or what comes to mind? Why? Do you prefer to be in a position of authority or under the authority of someone else? Who was/is the authority in your home? Who is their authority? What are some advantages of being under a good authority that truly cares for you? How would you describe God's authority to someone who has had unpleasant experiences with people misusing authority?

In today's culture, it may not be the wisest move to write a book with authority as the first topic covered. Yet, not only does it come first alphabetically, God's authority in heaven and on earth really is the foundation for making our journey home be a preparation for what we will experience when we arrive. Everything in heaven, even authority itself, exists in submission to Jesus so it may be a good idea to get used to that on our journey home. As you pray, ask God to help you live with the freedom that comes from recognizing His authority over everything. Pray that you would be a godly example of authority because of your submission to Him.

A Home with Authority

_____

_____

_____

_____

_____

_____

_____

_____

_____

_____

_____

_____

_____

_____

_____

_____

_____

_____

_____

Day Two

A Home

With Blessing

(Malachi 3:10)

A Home With Blessing

What is the greatest blessing that could be found in a home? How full of blessings would you say your life is? What would you do if you were to experience blessings that your home, or life, couldn't contain? Is it possible you already have been blessed to such an extent? What are you doing with the blessings God has already poured into your life? Would you live differently today if you were to recognize the blessings that are being poured out from within the home you're headed toward?

While the Bible teaches that it is more blessed to give than receive, our actions would say that most of us have a difficult time believing that. Far too often we think that God's blessings are meant solely for us when His intention is that we would allow them to flow through us and into the lives of others. If the home we're headed to is filled with more blessings than our lives can contain, then perhaps we out to be sharing those blessings as we take the journey home. As you pray, ask God to help you recognize His blessings in your life so you would be able to share them. Pray for a home that is a blessing to others.

A Home With Blessing

_____

_____

_____

_____

_____

_____

_____

_____

_____

_____

_____

_____

_____

_____

_____

_____

_____

_____

_____

Day Three

A Home

Of Citizenship

(Philippians 3:20)

A Home of Citizenship

What are some advantages of being a citizen where you currently live? What are your responsibilities as a citizen? When you consider the idea of citizenship, do you usually think more about your rights or your responsibilities? Why? Is a citizenship of a particular country helpful or harmful to a person who would seek to travel the world? In what ways? Does being a citizen of heaven make your journey on this earth easier or more difficult? In what ways?

Being a citizen means that you have a home where you belong and from which you can expect a certain amount of protection and rights, along with a level of responsibility. When I have travelled to foreign countries for prayer journeys, I've always understood that my U.S. citizenship carried with it some level of protection in certain places but also some increased danger in others. As a citizen of heaven on my journey home I have eternal protections but I also face danger because I journey through a foreign land. As you pray, ask God to confirm in you a citizenship in His kingdom that no one can take away.

A Home of Citizenship

_____

_____

_____

_____

_____

_____

_____

_____

_____

_____

_____

_____

_____

_____

_____

_____

_____

_____

_____

_____

Day Four

A Home Of

Completed Sacrifice

(Hebrews 9:24-25)

A Home of Completed Sacrifice

What are some things in your life that you would like to be finished with? Do you have projects, or tasks, which you find yourself doing over and over that you wish could be done once and for all? What sacrifices have you made to be where you are at in life? What sacrifices have others made on your behalf? Do you believe there will be further sacrifices necessary by yourself and others as you continue this journey of life? How does knowing you have a home where all sacrifice is complete help you as you journey toward that home?

I grew up in a home where the sacrifices made by my mom and dad on behalf of our family was so complete that I didn't recognize it or comprehend it until years later. There is great peace in knowing that all necessary sacrifice has been made so that our home can be filled fully with God's presence. As you pray, ask God to fill you with a confidence that He has called you to a home where all sacrifice has been made complete. Pray that your journey would be filled with hope as you trust in the sacrifice that has been made on your behalf.

A Home of Completed Sacrifice

_____

_____

_____

_____

_____

_____

_____

_____

_____

_____

_____

_____

_____

_____

_____

_____

_____

_____

_____

_____

_____

Day Five

A Home Of

Eternal Dwelling

(2 Corinthians 5:1)

A Home of Eternal Dwelling

How many places have you called home so far in your life? Do you think you will live at your current residence for the rest of your time on earth? Do you have a place where you like to vacation, or visit, that sometimes you wish you could just stay at forever? What things do you like most about that place? How would your life be lived differently if you kept your focus on the permanence of an eternal home? Does knowing you have an eternal home waiting help you in your life's journey?

I don't like change. While I do enjoy wandering and seeing new sights, even when I travel I seek out familiar places to eat and stay. But it is knowing that the comfort of home is waiting for me when the trip is over that helps me get through the unfamiliar parts of the journey. When I keep my eyes fixed on my eternal dwelling, I am able to endure the "light and momentary troubles" that exist in this life. As you pray, ask God to fill you with the confident expectation that He is preparing an eternal dwelling for you. Pray that you would live with endurance because of the hope that lies before you.

A Home of Eternal Dwelling

_____

_____

_____

_____

_____

_____

_____

_____

_____

_____

_____

_____

_____

_____

_____

_____

_____

_____

_____

_____

_____

Day Six

A Home

With Family

(Ephesians 3:14-15)

A Home With Family

What does your family name mean to you? Are you always proud of it? Why? Do you feel the same about your family now as you did five years ago? Ten years ago? Do you think you will feel the same way twenty years from now? Why? Are there people that feel more like family to you than actual family does? Why? What would you consider to be desirable qualities to have in a family? Would a family led by God have all of those qualities? How will living with those qualities help you as you journey toward home?

As those who have been adopted into God's family, He has given us a collection of brothers and sisters who share the family name "Christian". True family are those who look out for one another as they care for and nurture those who are in need. With God as our Father, we are part of a family that has full access to the family benefits of His glorious riches. As you pray, ask God to help you be the family member He desires for you to be. Pray that you would not only value being part of God's family, but that you would value each person that God has called into the family as your brothers and sisters.

A Home With Family

_____

_____

_____

_____

_____

_____

_____

_____

_____

_____

_____

_____

_____

_____

_____

_____

_____

_____

_____

_____

_____

Day Seven

A Home

With Feasting

(Matthew 8:11)

A Home With Feasting

What is your favorite food? What does the word feasting mean to you? What is the longest that you have intentionally gone without food? Have you ever gone without food simply because there wasn't any to be had? What role does food have in most celebrations you attend? Do you enjoy entertaining guests? How likely are you to ensure there will be plenty to eat when you invite people over? How would you describe the most fabulous feast you have ever been to?

It is difficult to imagine a wedding, graduation, or other significant celebration without an abundance of food. If you've ever had to go without simply because there wasn't any food or any money to obtain a meal, knowing that you are headed to a home with great feasting should be a great encouragement. God describes our eternal home as a celebration which includes feasting. As you pray, ask God to fill you with anticipation of what's to come. Pray that you would live life in a way that allows the people around you to have a glimpse of the feast God is preparing for those who complete the journey home.

A Home With Feasting

_____

_____

_____

_____

_____

_____

_____

_____

_____

_____

_____

_____

_____

_____

_____

_____

_____

_____

_____

_____

_____

Day Eight

A Home

Of Forgiveness

(2 Chronicles 7:14)

A Home of Forgiveness

Have you ever been wronged? Have you ever wronged someone else? How easy is it for you to forgive others? To forgive yourself? To seek forgiveness from others? How important is repentance to the topic of forgiveness? Is it possible to forgive someone who refuses to repent of their wrong? Is it possible to be forgiven if you refuse to repent of your wrong? What is the difference between those two situations? How would/does living in a home of forgiveness make you feel.

When I first got my driver's license, my parents said they would take my keys if I got into an accident. It wasn't long until I put my car in the ditch and needed towed out. When I got home, I handed my keys to my parents and went to bed. In the morning, when explanations could be given and lessons learned shared, my keys were returned to me and I experienced the joy of forgiveness. That wasn't the first, or last, time for the experience as I grew up in a home of forgiveness. As you pray, ask God to help you be a person who both gives and receives forgiveness. Pray that you would live as one prepared for a home of forgiveness.

A Home of Forgiveness

_____

_____

_____

_____

_____

_____

_____

_____

_____

_____

_____

_____

_____

_____

_____

_____

_____

_____

_____

_____

Day Nine

A Home

With Gifts

(John 3:27)

A Home With Gifts

What are some of the greatest gifts you have ever received? Who gave them to you? For what occasion? What do you feel are some of the greatest gifts you have ever given? Who did you give them to? Why? What made you believe they were so special? Which has greater meaning to you, a gift or the person who gives you that gift? What do you first think of when you consider a home with gifts? Are there other gifts that a home might have beyond the ones that first come to mind? What are they?

I still remember parts of my childhood and at that time of my life, a home with gifts meant Christmas or birthday. I still remember some of those gifts that I longed for, but I no longer have many of those gifts that seemed so important at the time. I do, however, still have the gifts of love, forgiveness, acceptance, and so many others that were given not only during my childhood but throughout my life. As you pray, ask God to help you recognize Him as the giver of all good gifts. Pray that you would place greater value on the gifts that He gives from His home than on the stuff that will perish.

A Home With Gifts

_____

_____

_____

_____

_____

_____

_____

_____

_____

_____

_____

_____

_____

_____

_____

_____

_____

_____

_____

_____

_____

Day Ten

A Home

With God

(Acts 17:24)

A Home With God

Who seemed to be the central presence in the home you grew up in? Who would you say is the central presence where you live now? If others live there as well, who would they say is central in the home? What would a home look like where God is present? What would the home's atmosphere feel like? Who would be central in that home? Is it possible for a person to be in charge of a home in a way that makes it known to others that God is present? How do you feel about a home with God even as you continue your journey?

I grew up in a home where my dad was very quiet but I always understood that he was in charge of the family and God was in charge of all of us. When I think of God and the various descriptions in the Bible of His dwelling, I am constantly in awe of the magnificence of being allowed in His presence for eternity. Not only that, but I can have a home with God even now as He makes His presence dwell within this jar of clay. As you pray, ask God to fill you with a desire to be at home with Him — not only when you finish this journey on earth but that each day of your life would be lived in His presence.

A Home With God

_____

_____

_____

_____

_____

_____

_____

_____

_____

_____

_____

_____

_____

_____

_____

_____

_____

_____

_____

Day Eleven

A Home

With Hope

(Colossians 1:5)

A Home With Hope

Have you ever been in a situation that seemed hopeless? Are you still in it or did you make it through? What got you through, or keeps you going? What role does encouragement, or the lack of it, at home have in your level of hope? Does having a place of hope help you endure difficult situations? How does the way you treat others change when you are filled with hope compared to when you feel hopeless? Does knowing you are headed toward a home filled with hope help you share that hope with others?

There have been various times in my life when I felt like I was completely in over my head in situations that appeared to have no way out. Some of those times were filled with such despair that it was only by holding on to the hope that I know awaits me in heaven that I managed to make it out of the darkness. A home of hope will help us get through some of the most difficult times of life. As you pray, ask God to fill you with the hope that is stored up for you in heaven. Pray that your home here on earth would be one filled with hope. Pray that you would freely share the hope you have in Christ with others.

A Home With Hope

_____

_____

_____

_____

_____

_____

_____

_____

_____

_____

_____

_____

_____

_____

_____

_____

_____

_____

_____

_____

Day Twelve

A Home

Of Influence

(Matthew 13:33)

A Home of Influence

What are some things that have had a huge influence in your life? Are those exact things noticeable in your life today or just the effects of their influence? What does it mean to you to have influence, or to be influenced? What kind of influence are you? Would the people around you agree? How has being a part of the kingdom of God influenced your life?

When I was a young boy learning my way around the kitchen, I made brownies one day but got stuck in understanding the ingredient list. I did okay until I reached a point where the recipe called for 1/4 teaspoon of BP. I had no idea what that stood for and decided to simply bypass that line as it was such a small amount — surely it wouldn't matter. Was I ever wrong! The brownies needed the influence of the Baking Powder to keep them from being the thin, rock hard substance they turned out to be. God says the kingdom of heaven is like that agent which works completely through our life to keep us from becoming a useless rock hard substance. As you pray, ask God to fill your life with the influence of your heavenly home. Pray that your influence would represent that home.

A Home of Influence

_____

_____

_____

_____

_____

_____

_____

_____

_____

_____

_____

_____

_____

_____

_____

_____

_____

_____

Day Thirteen

A Home

Of Innocence

(Matthew 19:14)

A Home of Innocence

What are some of your favorite childhood memories? What makes them so special? Are there things you know now, that if you knew then, would have made them less memorable? Why? Do you ever say or do things with pure and innocent motives that get made into something not so pure and innocent by others? How does that make you feel? How does a lack of innocence change the way you interact with people?

I can think of no scene that more vividly portrays the contrast between innocence and its loss, than the sin of Adam and Eve in the garden. To go in an instant from walking in innocence with one another and with God to, for the first time, feeling a sense of nakedness and hiding from one another and from God. Babies and very young children still have that innocence where they can live completely free and unhindered. Our home with God restores that innocence so that we have no need to hide from God or from anyone else. As you pray, ask God to help you walk with Him in complete innocence. Pray that you would be innocent of the things that are evil and excellent in the things that are good.

45

A Home of Innocence

_____

_____

_____

_____

_____

_____

_____

_____

_____

_____

_____

_____

_____

_____

_____

_____

_____

_____

_____

_____

_____

_____

Day Fourteen

A Home Of

Right Judgment

(Romans 1:18-19)

A Home of Right Judgment

Have you ever had someone pass judgment on you that was based on incorrect information? How did it make you feel? Do you tend to judge others based on information that may be incorrect or missing? How do you know? Have you ever had a judgment made against you that you didn't like but you knew they were right about it? How did you respond? Does knowing that God's standards are right and never-changing give you peace concerning His wrath?

While we may not mind undeserved credit, we definitely don't want undeserved blame. One thing we can count on in God's home is that His judgments will be always be right and always be based on truth. People, even you and I, can be very quick to pass judgment on others whether we have accurate information or not. As we journey towards our home in heaven, God wants us to seek Him for right judgments. As you pray, ask God to help you trust His judgments. Pray that you would turn to God when others make judgments about you that are inaccurate. Pray that the judgments you make in life would be based in the truth of God's Word.

A Home of Right Judgment

_____

_____

_____

_____

_____

_____

_____

_____

_____

_____

_____

_____

_____

_____

_____

_____

_____

_____

Day Fifteen

A Home With

Living Bread

(John 6:51)

A Home With Living Bread

What food do you find most satisfying? Why?
How often do you eat it? Do you think you
would get tired of it if it was all you ever had?
Why/why not? What things do you use to try
to satisfy the hungers you have in life? If you
could have a single thing that would
completely satisfy you, would you want it?
What would you do to obtain it? How does
knowing that Jesus is the living bread that can
sustain you each day help you as you journey
home?

I grew up in a home where there was little
money but we always had food and plenty of
homemade bread. When Jesus began talking
about being the bread of life, many began to
question how Jesus could be greater than the
manna Moses had given. Jesus responded
that Moses had only distributed bread which
had come from God and now He was the living
bread which came down from heaven. As you
pray, ask God to help you know Him as the
one who sustains your very life. Pray that you
would share with everyone the living bread
that God has given you in Jesus. Pray that
your home would be filled with the presence
of this bread.

A Home With Living Bread

_____

_____

_____

_____

_____

_____

_____

_____

_____

_____

_____

_____

_____

_____

_____

_____

_____

_____

_____

Day Sixteen

A Home

Of Majesty

(Hebrews 8:1-2)

Almost Heaven

A Home of Majesty

What image comes to your mind when you think of majesty? What does your dream home look like? Do you expect it will ever be a reality, or just a dream? Why? Is it possible to build a place with all of the best and most valuable materials, and it not be majestic? What does it take for something, or someone, to truly have majesty? Have you ever walked into a room or building and simply said, "Wow!" (In a good way)?   What was so impressive?

As I travel, there are times I walk into a building and am instantly impressed by the majesty that it presents. I am often more impressed by the majesty that I find out on a hike when I am surrounded by the true majesty of God's creation. While mankind has been gifted by God to build things which are beautiful and majestic, they all fall short of the majesty that flows from the very presence of God. As you pray, ask God to help you notice the glimpses of His majesty that He has surrounded you with. Pray that you would do your best each day to reflect the majesty that God has created in you. Pray that you would never tire of the "Wow!" factor.

54

A Home of Majesty

_____

_____

_____

_____

_____

_____

_____

_____

_____

_____

_____

_____

_____

_____

_____

_____

_____

_____

_____

_____

_____

_____

Day Seventeen

A Home

Of Obedience

(Matthew 7:21)

A Home of Obedience

How important is obedience in your home? In the home you grew up in? In the home you hope to have? How do you decide who/what to obey? Do you belong to any groups or organizations that requires adherence to their set of standards to belong? Why would you agree to obey their standards? How would you feel about someone that wanted the benefits of the group without following the rules of the group? How does a home of obedience provide a sense of belonging?

I grew up in a home where there was an expectation of obedience. While I didn't always obey perfectly, the expectation in place always helped me feel like I belonged. While obedience in my earliest years had a lot to do with a desire to avoid punishment, I eventually grew to where I obeyed out of love and respect. The home we are headed to is characterized by obedient children who love and respect their Father. As you pray, ask God to fill you with a desire to do what He says. Pray that you would repent of acts of disobedience and seek to make choices that honor the One you love. Pray that your obedience today would prepare you for home.

A Home of Obedience

_____

_____

_____

_____

_____

_____

_____

_____

_____

_____

_____

_____

_____

_____

_____

_____

_____

_____

_____

_____

Day Eighteen

A Home

Of Opportunity

(Matthew 13:31-32)

A Home of Opportunity

Have you ever missed an opportunity for something because you signed up too late or waited too long? How did you feel? How would it feel for someone to make room for you at a sold out event? How much potential do you think you have? How much do others think you have? What would God say is your potential? Who do you most often believe?

I grew up in a home where I was given great opportunities to reach my potential. I didn't always make the most of those opportunities, but they were always present. Because of that foundation, when Jesus teaches about the kingdom of heaven being like a mustard seed which starts out very small and grows into the largest of the garden plants, I am able to see the great opportunity that exists as a part of that kingdom. Regardless of our size, or the size we think we are, God gives us the opportunity as a part of His kingdom to grow into something that draws people to Himself. As you pray, ask God to help you make the most of the potential He has placed within you. Pray that you would see the seeds of the kingdom of heaven growing into a home that has room for all who would come.

A Home of Opportunity

_____

_____

_____

_____

_____

_____

_____

_____

_____

_____

_____

_____

_____

_____

_____

_____

_____

_____

_____

Day Nineteen

A Home

With Peace

(Luke 19:38)

A Home With Peace

How peaceful was the home you grew up in? How much peace exists in your current home? How would you rate the level of peace in the world? Why do you think that the level of peace is where it is? How important is peace to you? Would your activity as a peacemaker agree with your answer? What would it take to have greater peace in your life? In your home? Do you feel that you are at peace with God? Do you believe that He is at peace with you?

It seems that nearly everyone would like to have greater peace, but very few are willing to quit fighting in order to obtain it. Jesus taught that He did not come to earth to wield a sword, but to bring peace. He accomplished this through His death, burial and resurrection. In paying the penalty for our sin through His death, He made a way for there to be peace between us and God. In rising from the dead and defeating death, He made a way for that peace to be the core of our eternal home. As you pray, ask God to help you be a peacemaker. Pray that you would know the peace that comes down from heaven as you journey toward that eternal home.

A Home With Peace

_____

_____

_____

_____

_____

_____

_____

_____

_____

_____

_____

_____

_____

_____

_____

_____

_____

_____

Day Twenty

A Home

With Permanence

(1 Peter 1:3-5)

A Home With Permanence

What things have impressed you the most by how long they have lasted? What things have been the greatest disappointments by not lasting as you thought they should have? Have you ever headed somewhere with eager anticipation only to find out at your destination that the place no longer exists? How did you feel? How important is a sense of permanence in making you feel like you belong somewhere?

As a child, I never once worried about going home from school and not having a home to go to. While I realize now that the possibility existed for something to happen to it, I grew up with the security of having a home I believed to be permanent. Because of God's nature, I am assured that the heavenly home I am headed towards has a permanence that nothing can destroy. The hope I have on my journey to that home cannot be tarnished or diminished because I am confident my home will always be there. As you pray, ask God to fill you with the confidence of having a home that cannot be shaken. Pray that you would live life boldly, knowing that you are headed to a home of permanence.

66

A Home With Permanence

_____

_____

_____

_____

_____

_____

_____

_____

_____

_____

_____

_____

_____

_____

_____

_____

_____

_____

_____

_____

_____

Day Twenty-One

A Home

Of Rejoicing

(Luke 15:7)

A Home of Rejoicing

What has been the biggest celebration that you have been a part of? What was the cause for the rejoicing? How containable was the event? How happy are you when something good happens to a close friend or family member? Does their level of happiness influence how you respond? How difficult is it to put into practice God's command to rejoice always? Why? How does knowing that heaven is a home of rejoicing help you to rejoice on your journey?

A home of rejoicing has a tendency to attract people to it. In the midst of celebrating success and accomplishments, we want to share our joy with the people around us. Joy and laughter are contagious and especially so when we all have a reason to rejoice. There can be no greater reason for rejoicing and celebration than to finally arrive home to an eternity with God. As you pray, ask God to fill you with a spirit of joy as you journey toward His home filled with rejoicing. Pray that you would learn to rejoice always as you consider the home that awaits you. Pray that your home on earth would be filled with rejoicing because of your relationship with Christ.

A Home of Rejoicing

_____

_____

_____

_____

_____

_____

_____

_____

_____

_____

_____

_____

_____

_____

_____

_____

_____

_____

Day Twenty-Two

A Home

Of Rescue

(1 Thessalonians 1:9-10)

A Home of Rescue

Have you ever been stranded and have to call someone to come rescue you? How did you feel? How much time did you spend trying to figure your own way out of it before calling for help?   How difficult was it to admit you needed help? How did you feel about being rescued?   Was the relief of being rescued greater than the embarrassment of being stuck and in need of help? Does the attitude of the one rescuing you influence how you feel about needing rescued?

After spending a weekend teaching at a church, I headed home late at night only to have my car break down an hour into my six hour drive home. I popped the hood and fiddled around for a while before finally deciding it was hopeless and I needed rescued. I made a phone call to the family I knew in the town where I had been staying and was greatly relieved when they said they were on their way and even more relieved when their car pulled up behind me some time later. As you pray, ask God to help you comprehend your need to be rescued by Him. Pray that you would know the home you're headed to as one that has rescued you.

A Home of Rescue

_____

_____

_____

_____

_____

_____

_____

_____

_____

_____

_____

_____

_____

_____

_____

_____

_____

_____

_____

_____

Day Twenty-Three

A Home

Of Restoration

(Acts 3: 19-21)

A Home of Restoration

Is there a difference between repairing something and restoring it? What might that be? Have you ever had something of value that was worn out or broken that you had restored? How did the finished restoration make you feel? Are there things in your life that need restored? What would it take for that to happen? How much confidence would you have in something being fully restored if you knew the item's designer and creator were doing the restoration?

I am pretty good at breaking things and am improving at repairing them, but generally lack the ability to actually restore them. Many times when we mess up our life, we settle for a quick fix or simple repair when God wants to give us a full restoration. While God has made the way for us to be restored through the work of His Son; that work in us will not be fully complete until we are home with Him. As you pray, ask God to fill you with the desire to repent in order to bring about restoration. Pray that you would trust Him, as your designer and creator, to know how to fully restore you. Pray that God's restoration work in you would be brought to completion.

A Home of Restoration

_____

_____

_____

_____

_____

_____

_____

_____

_____

_____

_____

_____

_____

_____

_____

_____

_____

_____

_____

_____

_____

_____

Day Twenty-Four

A Home

Of Reward

(Luke 6:23)

A Home of Reward

Does it ever feel like your work and efforts in life go unappreciated? Are there times when your attempts to live in obedience to God are met with skepticism and ridicule? How easy is it to live a life devoted to Christ in your home? At your school? At your place of work? Are you joyful when people notice your walk with Christ, and hate you for it? Does the promise of a future reward help you endure difficult circumstances? How does a home of reward give you hope to persevere today?

Waiting under the best of circumstances is difficult for most people but when you add conflict and hardship, it is easy to lose sight of what we're waiting for and give up. It is by keeping our eye on the reward at the end that we are able to endure much. I know people who have stood outside all night in freezing temperatures just to receive the reward of a Black Friday sale. How much greater should our endurance be when we consider the reward waiting for us in heaven. As you pray, ask God to help you endure hardship as you look forward to your eternal reward. Pray that you would learn to rejoice in the midst of the testing that prepares you for home.

A Home of Reward

_____

_____

_____

_____

_____

_____

_____

_____

_____

_____

_____

_____

_____

_____

_____

_____

_____

_____

_____

Day Twenty-Five

A Home

Of Righteousness

(2 Peter 3:13)

A Home of Righteousness

When was the last time you did something wrong? Are you sure? Who defines right and wrong? How would your life be different if you could live with, and be surrounded by, complete righteousness? How upset do you get at the unrighteous acts of others? How does that compare with the way you view your own unrighteousness? Have you ever been a part of a group where, as much as humanly possible, all unrighteousness has been stripped away? What was it like?

In a world where lying, cheating, stealing, disobedience, and every other sin seek to pollute every aspect of our lives, it is comforting to know we are headed to a home of complete righteousness. This righteousness exists by the power of the blood of Jesus and the declaration of His Word. This same power declares you and I to be righteous when we are found in Christ. Our home today can show a glimpse of our future home when we live with a righteousness that is found in Christ. As you pray, ask God to help you daily put on His righteousness. Pray that you would reject sin and evil as you journey to a home that is filled with absolute righteousness.

81

A Home of Righteousness

_____

_____

_____

_____

_____

_____

_____

_____

_____

_____

_____

_____

_____

_____

_____

_____

_____

_____

_____

_____

Day Twenty-Six

A Home

Of Supremacy

(John 3:31)

A Home of Supremacy

Do you play or follow any particular sport or competitive activity? Who is number one in that particular thing? What did it take for them to achieve that ranking? What does it mean? How closely would you listen if the number one person in your occupational field offered to give you some advice? Why? Is there a difference between being supreme and having authority? Why? What effect does the misuse of the term supremacy by various individuals and groups have on your ability to see God as supreme?

When I think of heaven as being a home of supremacy, I think of Jesus being the One who was, who is, and who is to come. This home we are headed to is the dwelling of the One who was first — who is number one in the entire universe of existence. While there are some in this world who gain authority by force or deception, Jesus has authority by being. His supremacy in the home we are headed toward calls for us to listen to Him as we make the journey. As you pray, ask God to reveal Himself to you as the One who is supreme. Pray that your life today would reflect that supremacy as you live in obedience.

A Home of Supremacy

_____

_____

_____

_____

_____

_____

_____

_____

_____

_____

_____

_____

_____

_____

_____

_____

_____

_____

_____

_____

_____

Day Twenty-Seven

A Home

Of Transformation

(Matthew 18:3)

A Home of Transformation

How comfortable are you with change? Do you think the people closest to you would agree with your answer? Are there things about you that you would like to see changed? What is keeping that from happening? How has your life changed by being a follower of Christ? Are there people that have noticed a transformation in your life? Should they? How much transformation would it take for you to become like a little child? Where will you start? Who will help you?

As the disciples argued about who was the greatest, Jesus taught that entering the kingdom of heaven required a transformation of significant magnitude. We spend so much time wanting children to grow up and act like adults that we rarely comprehend the transformation that God desires in us. As we make the journey toward home, God wants to do His work of transformation in our lives. As you pray, ask God to lead you to a point of humility so that your heart can be transformed to become like that of a child. Pray that you would work on, and allow, the process of transformation to continue as you make your journey home.

A Home of Transformation

_____

_____

_____

_____

_____

_____

_____

_____

_____

_____

_____

_____

_____

_____

_____

_____

_____

_____

_____

_____

Day Twenty-Eight

A Home

With Treasure

(Luke 18:22)

A Home With Treasure

What do you value most in this life? What do you think the people closest to you would say you value most? Why? What would you do to get the thing you treasure most? Is there anything that you wouldn't give up? What does that say about what you really treasure? Have you ever saved up an amount of time and/or money in order to do something special? How did you feel about putting aside immediate desires in order to experience a treasured moment later? Was it worth it?

Many people save up money in order to have or do something at a later time. Typically our perceived value of what we're looking forward to will influence our seriousness in saving up for whatever it is. When God talks about heaven being a home with treasure, He does so as a reminder of the value it should have to us. When we view eternity with God to be the greatest treasure that could ever be obtained, it motivates us to loosen our grip on the stuff of this world that we are tempted to call treasures. As you pray, ask God to help you pursue a home with Him as the greatest treasure you could find. Pray that you would invest all you have in obtaining that treasure.

A Home With Treasure

_____

_____

_____

_____

_____

_____

_____

_____

_____

_____

_____

_____

_____

_____

_____

_____

_____

_____

_____

Day Twenty-Nine

A Home

Of Unity

(Ephesians 1:9-10)

A Home of Unity

What does unity mean to you? What things do you believe are necessary for unity to exist? What do you think are some of the reasons unity seems to be so elusive? Do you believe unity should be pursued at all costs? What might be some limits to the price of unity that might make it undesirable — or perhaps make it not be unity at all? What role does submission have when it comes to having a home of unity? How can your home today look more like the home of unity you are headed towards?

When the world speaks of unity, they are often actually referring to conformity. God says that heaven is a home of unity, not because we are all alike but because we are living our unique giftedness under one head — Jesus Christ. I like all of the parts of my truck to work in unity in order to transport me to where I want to go. I don't want a truck built out of parts that have all become the same — I want unique parts that are working together to accomplish the purpose of their designer. As you pray, ask God to help you live in unity with others as each of you accepts His headship over all things.

A Home of Unity

_____
_____
_____
_____
_____
_____
_____
_____
_____
_____
_____
_____
_____
_____
_____
_____
_____
_____
_____
_____
_____
_____
_____
_____

Day Thirty

A Home

Of Wisdom

(James 3:17)

A Home of Wisdom

Who is the wisest person you know? What makes you think that about them? Do you always make wise decisions? Why? Does advanced education always equal advanced wisdom? Why? What is the difference between the two? Have you ever been part of a home that lacked wisdom? What would, or did, it take for that to change? How desirable is a home of wisdom to you? How can you make your current home be more like the home of wisdom you are headed towards?

It appears that our culture has become so fixated with education that we no longer make much effort to pursue wisdom. It isn't that we should abandon our quest for education; rather we should add a deliberate pursuit of the wisdom that comes from God. God describes wisdom as a quality that flows from His character and is offered freely to all who would ask. As you pray, ask God to increase your wisdom as you grow in Christ. Pray that you would acknowledge God as your source of wisdom in all things. Pray that your home would be filled with a godly wisdom that comes from humility and represents the home you are headed toward.

A Home of Wisdom

_____

_____

_____

_____

_____

_____

_____

_____

_____

_____

_____

_____

_____

_____

_____

_____

_____

_____

_____

_____

Day Thirty - One

A Home

Of Worship

(Philippians 2:9-11)

A Home of Worship

What first comes to mind when you read the word, "worship"? Why? Would that first thought be accurate? Would it be complete? How often is the worship of God on your mind? Why? Is it possible to worship God without singing? Is it possible to sing worship songs without worshipping? What is required for worship to take place? Are you sure? What would a home of worship look and sound like to you? How can you make your current home be one of greater worship?

I'm not trying to reignite any old "worship wars" here, because frankly none of the ones I am familiar with really had much to do with worship. Our worship of God is our expression to Him of His worth. This ought to take place through every activity we are involved in and with every fiber of our being. God says that His Son was given a name above all others so that the very name of Jesus would receive worship in heaven, on earth, and even under the earth. As you pray, ask God to fill you with expressions of worship as you consider His Son, Jesus. Pray that you would not confine worship to any one place or activity but that your life would be worship.

A Home of Worship

Bonus Day

A Home

With God's Glory

(Acts 7:55)

A Home With God's Glory

Have you ever experienced a time when it seemed to you like an individual's presence completely filled a room? How did it make you feel? What do you think of when you consider God's glory? How overwhelming would a home with God's glory be? How comforting would it be? What would cause it to be more one than the other? How do the traits we've considered in the previous 31 days fit into a home with God's glory? How can your home today better reflect the glory of God in the home you are headed toward?

When I think of the glory of God, I first think about the description of God as being an all-consuming fire. Many times we connect that element of God with His judgment and wrath. While I think that is true, I also believe it describes the all-consuming nature of His glory. Heaven is a home where His presence cannot be hidden or ignored. His glory fills every part of this eternal home and of each person who dwells there. As you pray, ask God to so fill you with His glory that nothing could distract you from His presence. Pray that your journey home would be lived in pursuit of the glory of God filling you.

A Home With God's Glory

_____

_____

_____

_____

_____

_____

_____

_____

_____

_____

_____

_____

_____

_____

_____

_____

_____

_____

_____

_____